Nuclear Catastrophe in the Mideast

Nuclear Catastrophe in the Mideast

WIM MALGO

MIDNIGHT CALL PUBLICATIONS
POST OFFICE BOX 864
COLUMBIA, SOUTH CAROLINA 29202

©1981 COPYRIGHT BY
MIDNIGHT CALL PUBLICATIONS
POST OFFICE BOX 864
COLUMBIA, SOUTH CAROLINA 29202

Manufactured in the United States of America
ISBN 0-937422-22-3
Composition by Carolina Composing Room, Inc.

Contents

Chapter 1

The Crisis Between Israel and Syria
In the Light of Biblical Prophecy 11

Chapter 2

Libya & Ethiopia, Gomer & Togarmah
In the Light of the Prophetic Word....... 47

Chapter 3

Jordan, Saudi Arabia and Iraq
in Bible Prophecy 71

Introduction

Nuclear Catastrophe in the Mideast? Have we already reached that point? At the time of writing, not, but the preparations are in full swing. One thing is certain: the whole world feels the approaching nuclear catastrophe. This fearful and terrible holocaust predicted for us in Revelation 9, when one-third of humanity will be killed, has become a very possible reality today. This nuclear catastrophe has already taken more accurate visible forms in the Middle East. This in a reverse direction: Jerusalem destroyed a nuclear facility in enemy territory in the city of Baghdad. The International Press has discussed and reported the details of Israel's attack on Iraq's nuclear facilities in detail. No doubt, Iraq's desire to possess nuclear weapons has been postponed. Now, the question arises: "who is in the possession of nuclear weapons?" In this book, we point to the fact that, for instance, Pakistan, Libya and Iraq are attempting to possess nuclear weapons at all costs. It is our belief that Israel does possess nuclear bombs. Leading Israeli political personalities have pointed out publicly "they will not be the first to use nuclear weapons in that region."

In the end-battle of the nations, nuclear weapons will be used according to the Prophetic Word. The prophet Zechariah describes very graphically what will happen to those nations who will march with force against Jerusalem. In chapter 14:12, he describes the result from a nuclear explosion on the enemies of Jerusalem, "And this shall be the plague wherewith the Lord will smite all the people that have fought against Jerusalem; their flesh shall consume away while they stand upon their feet, and their eyes shall consume away in their holes, and their tongue shall consume away in their mouth." From the Bible, we know that the center of God's dealing is Israel. In Romans 5:20 it says, "But where sin abounded, grace did much more abound." To transfer this to Israel, we can say of the deathly threat of the enemies to Israel is becoming stronger, but the Godly promises of protection are much mightier, nevertheless! Israel will, under all circumstances survive because the Messiah is coming and He is the one who has the world in His hand; nothing is out of His control. Indeed, we can say "Nuclear Catastrophe in the Mideast" because the Lord will judge, through the element of fire (compare Isaiah 66:16, Joel 19:30-31, II Peter 3:10-12). The end of this judgment, however, is that Israel will be protected throughout by the Lord (compare Joel 3:16).

With this book, we intend also to show the prophetic background and the origin of the enmity against Israel in the light of the Bible. Because the reasons lie much deeper than we read about in secular history or current news reports, it must be uncovered through the Word of prophecy (compare Isaiah 61:60). In short, the power over the world is being handed back to Israel — it is being taken away from the nations. This is rather natural for the Prince of Peace, Jesus Christ, will come again soon and will establish his Kingdom of Peace in Jerusalem and rule from there the entire world (compare Isaiah 2:2-4, Micah 4:1-5)!

The New Testament, too, speaks of a nuclear catastrophe as we read about it in II Peter 3:10, "But the day of the Lord will come as a thief in the night; in the which the heavens shall pass away with a great noise, and the elements shall melt with fervent heat, the earth also and the works that are therein shall be burned up." That is a summarizing description of the coming judgment to the final end. The God of the Universe will protect His own people, Israel, throughout; He even guarantees it in His Word. The whole universe will cease to exist before He will reject Jerusalem or Israel (compare Jeremiah 33:25-26). The deeper purpose of this book is to revive the hearts of believers with the hope of the soon returning Lord. Indeed, our Lord is coming soon!

September, 1981

Chapter 1

The Crisis Between Israel and Syria In the Light of Biblical Prophecy

"The Lord our God spake unto us in Horeb, saying, Ye have dwelt long enough in this mount: turn you, and take your journey, and go to the mount of the Amorites, and unto all the places nigh thereunto, in the plain, in the hills, and in the vale, and in the south, and by the sea side, to the land of the Canaanites, and unto Lebanon, unto the great river, the river Euphrates. Behold, I have set the land before you: go in and possess the land which the Lord sware unto your fathers, Abraham, Isaac, and Jacob, to give unto them and to their seed after them" (Deuteronomy 1:6-8).

We cannot behave as though nothing is happening in the world today; and we cannot overlook God's accelerated actions in the Middle East, especially concerning Israel. I think one of the biggest mistakes the Church makes is to speak about everything except what God is saying through world events today. Thus we are going to look into the crisis between Israel and Syria, especially since we are now hearing more and more about it through the mass media. Let's look at it now, however, in light of the prophetic Word.

To begin with, I would like to say the following: since the founding of the state of Israel in 1948, nothing takes place in the Middle East or in the world which is not directly or indirectly connected with the fulfillment of the prophetic Word. Israel is, if I may put it this way, the channel through which the prophetic Word has begun to be fulfilled, including the above text which is extremely topical. However, we must realize that such contrasting powers, which are colliding particularly in the Middle East since the restoration of the State of Israel, were never before in action. The reappearance of Israel has made centuries-old dormant hostility toward this chosen people and land flare up. This is because the ancient prophecies of the Bible have suddenly come to pass. Thus the crisis between Israel and Syria, which is now coming to a climax, has a tremendous prophetic-historical background.

The Prophetic Word and its fulfillment is an integrated part of Israel. In this picture, we see Israel's Prime Minister, Menachem Begin, praying at the Wailing Wall.

We, as New Testament believers, have a fanatic ancient enemy. He is and has been very active in my life and yours ever since we were raised with Christ and we started to follow Jesus. The more we become a part of fulfilled prophecy, in that Jesus Christ becomes visible in us, the more the enemy will be actively against us.

It is not to be supposed that the present day Syrians, who are the most fanatically opposed against Israel, can analyze the deep ancient roots of their hatred. They view present day Israel as a cancer in the Arab body. Some time ago, I read of a Syrian army captain who lectured one of his subordinates in the motivation for the war against Israel. He said to him, "Give me your hand." Then he took a knife and said, "Hold out your open hand. Your fingers now represent our individual Arab states. We are not united." He then placed the knife point in the palm of the man's hand which promptly closed in pain around the blade of the knife. The captain said, "Do you see? Israel is the knife-point in the Arab body, and in this way we Arabs are drawn together and become united in our rejection of Israel."

This is what is taking place in our day. The

Syrian Sam-6 missles in Lebanon. These very effective surface-to-air missles are ready, aimed at Israel.

Syrians have this hatred, but they are not able to analyze it. Why is it to Syria's advantage that the crisis with Israel is increasing in these days? It is because Syria is liberated from increasing isolation in the Arab world. Syria, who was in isolation from the Arab states for some time, is drawing nearer to unity today. I am thinking of Saudi-Arabia and Jordan, who, although were mortal enemies before are now on Syria's side.

Thus, we, as the Church, the body of Jesus Christ, must beware of negative bloc-building such as we see in the Arab world. Negative bloc-building is unity, but not in Jesus Christ the crucified One. It is unity in the weakening of the existing spiritual unity, in the refusal to be sanctified. The more we have this positive unity in the Lord Jesus Christ, the more the Lord will be able to bless us. This is the unity of Acts 2:1 and 4, *"They were all with one accord...and they were all filled with the Holy Ghost."* But woe betide us if we build a negative, destructive unity, even together with one person, against those who are chosen of God, as we see this in the Arab world which is united against Israel.

On the other hand, I believe that Israel

herself is not able to realize or analyze the centuries-old hatred that is concentrated against her. This is no new crisis, my friends, it has a background, and there is much history behind it. I think Israel is so unaware of this because so few people in Israel know their own Bibles. In just the same way, many children of God are ignorant regarding the things that happen to them. We are tried and tempted and thoughts are conceived in our hearts; we are tossed to and fro and we only see people before us and do not realize that

Two fundamental issues are at stake in the Middle East. One: the people of Israel. Picture shows some 100,000 supporters of Begin before the election in June, 1981.

Two, the physical land of Israel in its boundaries according to God's Word. Picture shows the city of Haifa.

something quite different is behind it all. As Paul says in Ephesians 6:12, *"For we wrestle not against flesh and blood, but against principalities, against powers, against the rulers of the darkness of this world, against spiritual wickedness in high places."* And in James 1:12 we read, *"Blessed is the man that endureth temptation: for when he is tried, he shall receive the crown of life, which the Lord hath promised to them that love him."*

There are two factors in this crisis in the Middle East: first are the nations, Israel and Syria; and second, the land of Israel. Those who think that in the Middle East today, the

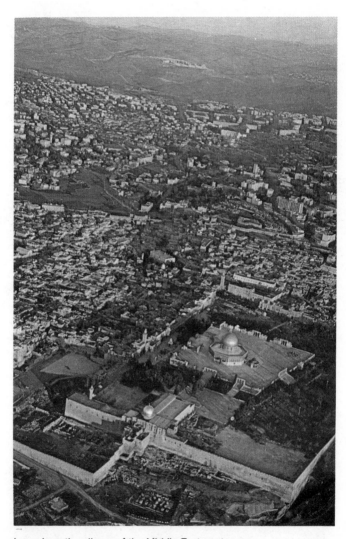
Jerusalem, the climax of the Middle East controversy.

problem is a battle between Syria and "Christians" in Lebanon (whereby we must remember that today the term "Christian" is a very loose one which can be applied to Roman Catholics, Greek-Orthodox, Protestants, etc.) in which Israel is helping the "Christians" and the P.L.O. is helping Syria, those who think this are greatly in error. That is what the politicians are doing. The position changes from year to year in this respect. I remember in 1975, when civil war broke out in Lebanon and the Syrians murdered the P.L.O. adherents. That has changed today!

Let's take a look at the roots of these two nations, Israel and Syria. They have a common ancestor, and I am not speaking of Abraham. Abraham is the father of Israel and the father of all them that believe, father of the circumcision; he is called "father" seven times in Romans chapter 4. But I want to go back even further. Israel and Syria, in contrast to all other Arab states, have *one* common father. We can read this in Genesis 11:27, *"Now these are the generations of Terah: Terah begat Abram, Nahor, and Haran; and Haran begat Lot. And Haran died before his father Terah in the land of his nativity, in Ur of the Chaldees. And Abram and Nahor took them wives: the name of Abram's wife was Sarai; and the name of Nahor's wife Milcah."* So Abram and Nahor had the same father, and that was Terah; and Nahor, Abraham's brother, is the father of the Syrians. We read in Genesis 22:20-21, *"And it came to pass after these things, that it was told Abraham, saying, Behold, Milcah, she hath also born children unto thy brother Nahor; Huz his firstborn, and Buz his brother, and Kemuel the father of Aram."* Aram is another name for Syria. So we have Abraham, the father of the nation of Israel and Nahor, married to Milcah, the father of the nation of Syria. They both have one father: Terah. The Syrians, in contrast to all other Arabs, are pure Semites, which is their great advantage. Most of the other Arab nations descend from Ishmael, and that is a mixture. Abraham took an Egyptian maid to be his wife, and Ishmael was born out of this union. Ishmael also united himself with Gentiles, while in the case of Syria we have a clear Semitic line directly from Nahor, Abraham's brother. Terah had two sons then, Abraham and Nahor; the third was Haran, but he died. Now the Lord's call at that time was not to Abraham alone, but to all of his family. We see this from the direction of Terah's journey. We read in Genesis 11:31, *"And Terah took Abram his son, and Lot the son of Haran his son's son, and Sarai his daughter-in-law, his son Abram's wife; and they went forth with them from Ur of the Chaldees, to go into the land of Canaan; and they came unto Haran, and dwelt there."* They were going in the right direction — toward Canaan. We see that although the Lord does not speak here, or perhaps was not able to speak because they did not understand, His Spirit was leading Terah and his family in the right direction, toward Canaan, the wonderful Promised Land.

However, we see a rift in the family here already. Who is missing in verse 31? Nahor! Thus we begin to see the background of the crisis in the Middle East. Why was Nahor missing? We know one thing from Joshua 24:2, which is that Nahor committed idolatry as did Abraham. But Nahor did not heed God's call. The second tragedy was that Terah also got no further and he did not reach the goal. There are many people who have started out to follow Jesus, they have heard His call, and started off in the right direction, but they got stuck somewhere. Why? Verse 31 of Genesis 11 says, *"And they went forth with them from Ur of the Chaldees, to go into the land of Canaan; and they came unto Haran, AND DWELT THERE."* They got stuck there and went no farther. The name "Terah" strangely enough, means "loiterer." Terah must have been the sort of person who could not completely let go of everything. He took Abraham with him, who was about seventy years old; and he took his wife, his possessions, and his nephew Lot — it seems that Nahor did not want to go with him — and he journeyed toward Canaan, but he got stuck. And as long as Terah the father was stuck, Abraham was also stuck. What had to happen before Abraham could go on? Terah had to die. Terah, who is a picture of the "old-man" in us, who holds up things, lived to a ripe old age, as we read in the last words of Genesis chapter 11, *"And the days of Terah were two hundred and five years: and Terah died in Haran."* The next chapter then begins with the words, *"Now the Lord had said unto Abram, Get thee out of thy country, and from thy kindred, and from thy father's house, unto a land that I will shew thee."* It is as though the Lord is saying here, "Now you can proceed, Abraham! You have waited long enough!" The loiterer was dead. We hear no more of Nahor, however, until Genesis 22:20-21 which we have already read, where Abraham receives a birth announcement, *"And it came to pass after these things, that it was told Abraham, saying, Behold, Milcah, she hath also born children unto thy brother Nahor; Huz his firstborn, and Buz his brother, and Kemuel the father of Aram."* Syria is often translated as "Aram," as we have already seen, but it is the same country. We see later on in the Bible how Nahor was entangled in idolatry, for instance in Judges 10:6, *"And the children of Israel did evil again in the sight of the Lord, and served Baalim, and Ashtaroth, and THE GODS OF SYRIA..."* Nahor became a curse to the descendants of Abraham. Balaam, who wanted to curse Israel but could not, was also a Syrian, a descendant of Nahor. Nahor preferred to remain behind in Ur of the Chaldees instead of going with Abraham his brother. He is, I repeat, the father of the present day Syrians, and the meaning of his name is twofold: "snorting" or "snoring." This was a hindrance in his inner attitude toward the descendants of his brother Abraham. It was a family affair. Nahor was envious, and it was this that made him blind. He must have seen how Abraham was blessed beyond measure because he followed God to the unknown land, while he, Nahor, was stuck in Ur and things were not going well for him. He served other gods, and envy and rage filled his heart.

These are the two negative characteristics of many members of the New Covenant who

Remnants of Ur, from where Abraham departed to the Promised Land.

have not followed the Lord where He led them, but preferred to serve the idols of materialism, etc., and who, like Nahor, see how their Christian brethren are blessed of the Lord, and they react by "snorting," and are full of envy. I have had my personal experience of this, and if envy could kill a person I would have died a thousand times. "Snorting" — that describes the fanatical anger of the Syrians. When we compare them to the surrounding nations, such as Egypt, who has a tendency toward peace, Jordan and Saudi-Arabia, Syria is the state which is the most irreconcilable. The New Testament Nahors are also the sleepers, the "snorers." These people are the greatest danger for the spiritual seed of Abraham, which is the Church, just as Nahor's descendants, the Syrians, are the greatest danger for the natural seed of Abraham, Israel, up to the present day. Israel's history shows this! It is a history of continual war with Syria. Yet Syria was never really free. Envious people are never really free; they have complexes and they are introspective. Syria was included by Tiglath-Pileser in the Assyrian World Empire in 740 B.C. From 625-560

B.C., Syria was a part of the Chaldean-Babylonian Empire; and from 560-332 B.C., Syria was under Persian rule. Alexander the Great, a Greek, also ruled over it for a short period, a year, after which he died. Then from 64 B.C. until 395 A.D., Syria was a province of the Roman Empire and afterward it was swallowed up by the Arabs. Syria is still not free today in 1981! Behind Syria is the greatest shadow of the Soviet Union, and it has to do what the Soviet Union wants. There is also a spiritual application in this. As long as Israel committed idolatry she was not free; she was ruled over by her enemies. And as long as you cling to other gods besides your faith in Jesus Christ you will not be free. You will be ruled by the enemy for, *"He that committeth sin is of the devil"* (I John 3:8) and *"Whosoever committeth sin is the servant of sin"* (John 8:34).

To return to Nahor, the father of Syria, he also heard God's call to Terah's family, but did not give up his idols. God's call included him; he was Abraham's brother and he obviously walked and talked with him. Abraham heeded God's call, but Nahor clung to his gods. I am reminded here of Paul's words in I Thessalonians 1:9, *"...how ye turned to God from idols to serve the living and true God."* There are many Nahors today who say they are serving the living God but they have not given up their idols. This is their tragedy; that is why they make no progress. For when they see the "Abrahams" and the "Israels" progressing, their hearts are filled with anger. They slander others and thoughts arise in their hearts which are solely the product of their own imagination — because they are "Nahors," "Syrians."

The centuries-old story of Syria and Israel is one of blood and tears; and today, the spirit of Nahor — "snorting" — is becoming more and more perceptible in Israel. We see from the following press report just how dangerous the so-called "missile crisis" is and how it is coming to a climax:

> The evacuation of 65 relatives of Soviet diplomats in Beirut, the discontinuation of flights to Beirut of the Saudi-Arabian Airline, the shooting down of another unmanned Israeli reconnaissance aircraft (the third), caused the Middle East crisis barometer to rise. Begin's demand to remove, within the framework of the restoration of the previous conditions, also the missiles from the proximity of the Syrian border, was called a declaration of war by the Syrian Press.

The Euphrates River in Iraq. According to the Word of God, this is the north border of Israel.

Israel's attacks had already begun a day or two later. Apart from the exciting prophetic fact that in Lebanon, very near to Israel, the Libyans are suddenly intervening, this is a literal fulfillment of prophecy. The Soviet Union is behind it, but according to Ezekiel 38:5, the Persians (Iran), the Ethiopians (who are already contaminated by Communism), and the Libyans will march with her — and the Libyans are already there! Israel's Prime Minister Begin was recently asked at a press conference why Israel is launching another attack when she is in such a crisis and he replied, "There are Libyans in Lebanon who are just asking to be destroyed." The uncanny thing about this crisis is that everyone is talking of a war which nobody really wants. Neither the Syrians or Russians, nor the Israelis and Americans, nor by any means the Lebanese, upon whose bloody back this conflict is being fought. None of them want this war, yet it is leading up to a means of communication between the parties concerned. Nobody speaks about the actual reason that there must be a war. In the same way there are many family conflicts, even among Christians, which are recognized as conflicts; but the deep, hidden cause of them is not recognized. We have known the political facts for a long time: behind the disguise of the "peace keeping force," Syria is attempting to establish herself once and for all in Lebanon. She would like to become "Great Syria;" she wants to annex Lebanon. On the

Mediterranean Sea

Beirut

22,000 Syrian troops occupy
Beirut and area to east
and southeast.

Phalangists—Christian rightists—
battle Syrian soldiers for control.

U.N. troops harassed
by both Christians
and Palestinians.

25,000 armed Palestinian guerrillas
roam southern Lebanon.

Christian rightists proclaim "Free
Lebanon" along southern border.

LEBANON

Zahle

Bekaa Valley

Sidon

Tyre

SYRIA

ISRAEL

Scale of miles
0   25

USN&WR map

Not only a part, but all of Lebanon belongs to Israel.

other hand, Israel feels threatened. But, my friends, we must see the second reason; namely, that this war has to break out sooner or later.

I have named two nations as the first reason. Now we come to the land. Let us turn again to our text in Deuteronomy 1:7, *"Turn you, and take your journey, and go to the mount of the Amorites, and unto all the places nigh thereunto, in the plain, in the hills, and in the vale, and in the south, and by the sea side, to the land of the Canaanites, and unto Lebanon, unto the great river, the river Euphrates."* The Euphrates flows through Syria, through Iraq, and includes the whole of Lebanon. That is the northern border of Israel. Verse 8 continues, *"Behold, I have set the land before you: go in and possess the land which the Lord sware unto your fathers, Abraham, Isaac and Jacob, to give unto them and to their seed after them."* Notice that it does not say the Lord promised, but the Lord *sware* unto your fathers. My friends, this is the background of the crisis in our day. It is not the world-political norms which are decisive, nor the press commentaries. The world-political opinion is that Israel must withdraw and practice so-called "moderation." But what is decisive is God's oath in which He also included Lebanon. I know that such Bible verses are against all political logic and doctrine, but if we follow it, we have chosen the way of truth. Only God's Word is the truth. It is interesting to see that Israel is compared three times to Lebanon even in the Old Testament. For instance, we have Hosea 14:5-7, *"I will be as the dew unto Israel; he shall grow as the lily, and cast forth his roots as Lebanon. His branches shall spread, and his beauty shall be as the olive tree, and his smell as Lebanon. They that dwell under his shadow shall return; they shall revive as the corn, and grow as the vine: the scent thereof shall be as the wine of Lebanon."* Here we see the inner connection between Lebanon and Israel. The state, the mountains of Lebanon, where Israel and Syria are now confronting one another lies to the north of Israel. The name "Lebanon" means "white mountain" in English. As we know it from the world-political scene, the confrontation area between Israel and Syria is about 105 miles long, alongside the Mediterranean coast, between Tyre and Arvad, and to the east of

The mountains of Lebanon.

this lies the smaller mountain range called,
strangely enough, Anti-Lebanon. I want to
emphasize here that not just parts of Lebanon
are promised to Israel, but *the whole of
Lebanon*. This is written in Joshua 13:5, *"And
the land of the Giblites, and ALL LEBANON,
toward the sunrising, from Baal-gad under
mount Hermon unto the entering into Hamath."*
We can also read Deuteronomy 11:24-25 in this
connection, *"Every place whereon the soles of
your feet shall tread shall be yours: from the
wilderness and Lebanon, from the river, the*

river Euphrates, even unto the uttermost sea shall your coast be. There shall no man be able to stand before you: for the Lord your God shall lay the fear of you and the dread of you upon all that land that ye shall tread upon, as he hath said unto you." In my opinion, it could not be clearer! But today, the norm of the Scriptures is lost. With this statement if Scripture, however, we have one of the main reasons for the threatening war between Syria and Lebanon. It is good and comforting to know that the future will be different, as we read in Isaiah when Assyria (that is, Syria), Egypt, and Israel will serve the Lord together. This will be when the Lord has returned. *"In that day shall there be a highway out of Egypt to Assyria and the Assyrian shall come into Egypt, and the Egyptian into Assyria, and the Egyptians shall serve with the Assyrians. In that day shall Israel be the third with Egypt and with Assyria, even a blessing in the midst of the land: whom the Lord of hosts shall bless, saying, Blessed be Egypt my people, and Assyria the work of my hands, and Israel mine inheritance,"* (Isaiah 19:23-25). This will all come to pass, but now we see the opposite. That is why Lebanon is always a symbol of great and glorious things in the Bible. Lebanon belongs to Israel according to His promise; but also because, as we have already seen, she has an inner connection with the people of Israel. For instance, we have the promise of Isaiah 35:2, which is similar to the text we have just read in Hosea, *"It shall blossom abundantly, and rejoice even with joy and singing: the glory of Lebanon shall be given into it, the excellency of Carmel and Sharon, they shall see the glory of the Lord, and the excellency of our God."* The prophet

Zechariah calls Jerusalem and the Holy Land "the burned country of Lebanon." We read in Zechariah 11:1-2, *"Open thy doors, O Lebanon, that the fire may devour thy cedars. Howl, fir tree; for the cedar is fallen; because the mighty are spoiled: howl, O ye oaks of Bashan; for the forest of the vintage is come down."* From verse 6 of the same chapter, we see that the "land of Israel" is meant here in this pronouncement of judgment. There are many passages in the Bible (Jeremiah 22:6) where Israel's identity with Lebanon is emphasized. Moreover it was Moses' dying wish, in Deuteronomy 3:25, that he might see the land of Lebanon, *"I pray thee, let me go over, and see the good land that is beyond Jordan, that goodly mountain, and LEBANON."* The mountains of Lebanon were famous, of course, for their cedars. The cedar is a very interesting tree; a one-hundred year old cedar, for example, has a trunk which is no thicker than a man's thigh above the knee. They become up to 3,000 years old, and they stand as evergreen memorials in Lebanon, if they have not been cut or burned down. Almost every Saturday evening I read Psalm 92 with my family in preparation for the Lord's day, where the believer is likened to a cedar in Lebanon. Verses 12-14, *"The right-eous shall flourish like the palm tree: he shall grow like a cedar in Lebanon. Those that be planted in the house of the Lord shall flourish*

The famous Cedars of Lebanon. ▼ ▶

in the courts of our God. They shall still bring forth fruit in old age; they shall be fat and flourishing." This is why those who are planted in the house of the Lord remain young! We are going toward eternal youth; and although our outward man is perishing, our inward man is renewed from day to day.

In II Chronicles, we read that King Solomon used cedars from Lebanon to build the temple, and it especially thrilled me to read that the Holy of Holies containing the art of the

Israel's most deadly enemies, the PLO terrorists. But they are foreigners in that land.

covenant was also built of cedar wood.

This wounded country of Lebanon, then, which is going through such suffering, belongs to Israel, according to God's promise. He has not only promised this, but He has also done it, in that He identifies her with the city of Jerusalem, the land of Israel, His house, the Holy of Holies where His presence was, and even with the believers of the New Covenant. This mighty, prophetic fact enables us to see the battles in Lebanon among foreigners — Arabs against Christians, Moslems against Christians and against Israel — in a new light. It is just the same with the battle within us which is described in Galatians 5:17, *"For the flesh lusteth against the Spirit, and the Spirit against the flesh."* As long as the Spirit of the Lord does not reign in us, this battle will continue. The foreigners in Lebanon, the Syrians, the Moslems, the so-called Christians who come from Ishmael and Esau, are not the heirs of the country. They are tearing one another to pieces over a land that is not theirs. It is interesting when we recall the time before World War I, when Lebanon was partly Turkish, but the Turks were not the heirs of the land. Then in the twenties, the French

American special negotiator, Mr. Habib, with Syrian President Assad. His mission was unsuccessful because Lebanon does belong to Israel according to the Bible.

came as the mandate power to Syria. They were also not the heirs, and had to relinquish it. The present state of Lebanon has been in existence since the year 1920, and they have thus had 61 years to establish themselves, and they were apparently very successful in the attempt. Before the civil war, Lebanon was called the oriental Switzerland. But this mixture of Moslems, Christians, Arabs of Armenian, and Kurdist origin, is not the heir of this country. Thus since 1975 this poor country has been torn apart by civil war. Therefore we must see the bloody battles and a possible war between Israel and Syria as a desperate fight against the true heir, which is Israel. It is strange, but the more the state of Israel grows, despite the fact that they are being tossed to and fro by internal and external crises, the more her enemies tear one another to pieces. Before the civil war in Lebanon, that is before 1975, there was a political and religious balance of power. The population of Lebanon at that time comprised 53.7% "Christians" and 45.3% Moslems. This fact is very relevant, for here lies the basic cause of the hopeless situation in Lebanon: her divided nature. And it is this divided nature toward Israel that is her downfall; for Lebanon belongs to Israel according to the promise and was the only Arab state which, if any country, would make peace with Israel — it would be her. Lebanon did not take part in any of the four wars in the Middle East. She was neutral and often sympathized with Israel. In the Yom Kippur War, the Israeli Air Force was able to fly unhindered over Lebanon to Syria. She instinctively felt her bond with Israel, yet already in 1948, at the founding of the state of Israel, she did not have the inner strength to stand with Israel. And now in her desperate position, prominent Lebanese have often declared, "Let us seek refuge in Israel." But this decision is too late and it cannot heal Lebanon's terrible wound. The strange phenomenon is that the common people of

Lebanon have been coming over the border to Israel to seek help and healing for their wounds — and they find it, at the "good fence," the open border. Wounded are taken to Israeli hospitals in Israeli ambulances. An Israeli soldier who saw how the Lebanese were helped exclaimed, "My health insurance does not do that much for me!" When they are healed, however, they return to their "hell" in Lebanon. That report shattered me, my friends, because Lebanon's situation is an unmistakably clear prophetic warning to us. This division in Lebanon, which is being torn apart by her enemies who do not belong there, shows us how perilous it is for us to be inwardly divided toward the God of Israel, toward Jesus Christ. Permit me to tell you that if you are inwardly divided toward the Lord who bought you at such a price, you do not need to be surprised that you are gradually being inwardly torn apart by the devil. Everything that happens in the Middle East, in and around Israel, is an example to us, according to I Corinthians 10:11. Your trouble is your divided heart toward the Lord, like Lebanon, who belongs to Israel according to the promise but is divided in her attitude toward Israel — that is her downfall!

The results of this are devastating — in your life, also. Whoever does not have a clear "No" to sin and a clear "Yes" to Jesus Christ will see how the enemy tears him apart. May I give you one last illustration concerning Lebanon?

When we look at a map of that country, we see the mountain range of the Anti-Lebanon to the east, which leads up to Mount Hermon. Yet the Anti-Lebanon is not Mount Hermon. It almost looks as though it is, but it is not. It is

The mountains of Hermon are connected with the mountains of Anti-Lebanon.

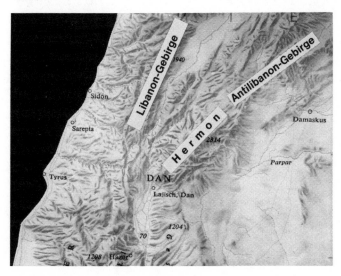

Mr. Habib in discussion with Israel's Prime Minister, Menachem Begin.

almost as though the geographic situation of Lebanon is pointing to her divided nature. My brothers and sisters, let me warn you now: do not permit the Antichrist in your heart beside Christ, like Lebanon and Anti-Lebanon. You see the result of this in Lebanon. The whole situation there is a New Testament warning to us, as it is written in James 5:8, *"Be ye also patient; stablish your hearts: for the coming of the Lord draweth nigh."* Do you know how your heart can be established? We find the answer in II Chronicles 16:9, *"The eyes of the Lord run to and fro throughout the whole earth, to shew himself strong in the behalf of them whose heart is perfect toward him."*

Chapter 2

Libya & Ethiopia, Gomer & Togarmah In the Light of the Prophetic Word

"And the word of the Lord came unto me, saying, Son of man, set thy face against Gog, the land of Magog, the chief prince of Meshech and Tubal, and prophesy against him, and say, Thus saith the Lord God; Behold, I am against thee, O Gog, the chief prince of Meshech and Tubal: and I will turn thee back, and put hooks into thy jaws, and I will bring thee forth, and all thine army, horses and horsemen, all of them clothed with all sorts of armour, even a great company with bucklers and shields, all of them handling swords: Persia, Ethiopia, and Libya with them; all of them with shield and helmet: Gomer, and all his bands; the house of Togarmah of the north quarters, and all his bands: and many people with thee" (Ezekiel 38:1-6).

It is quite fascinating to see that Libya and Ethiopia are mentioned by name in the Bible.

These verses speak about the attack of Russia and her satellites on Israel; they will cover the land like a cloud. "The chief prince of Meshech and Tubal" refer, of course, to Moscow and Tobolsk.

Libya

Libya was Turkish until 1912; from then until 1947 she was more or less Italian. Then on December 24, 1951 she became a federated kingdom under King Idris. A few years later, on September 1, 1969 he was overthrown and Libya became an Arab Republic under the famous or better, infamous Colonel Gadhafi. We know that since the Arab conquest of North Africa, Libya belongs to the Islam world, but simultaneously, as we have just read in verse 4 of Ezekiel 38, she is expressly mentioned in the Bible as being an ally of the Soviet Union, and therefore a double wave of hatred and destruction toward Israel emanates from her. On one hand, there is the spirit of the Soviet Union, one could say the anti-God movement; and on the other hand, there is the spirit of Islam, the anti-Christian movement. It is no wonder that Libya has already become an army camp with a mass weapon arsenal of the Soviet Union. This is a contradiction; when you think that Gadhafi and his followers are fanatic Moslems, yet it is very strange that they at the same time collaborate with world Communism. They are united only in their common goal, the destruction of Israel, just as Pilate and Herod became friends over their mutual rejection of Jesus.

Libya is a great threat to Israel, as you will bee by reading the following press reports:

German rockets for Gadhafi. Secret contact confirmed: The Munich firm OTRAG (Orbital Transport and Rocket Co. Ltd.) is building missile carriers for nuclear warheads in Libya. The "object" was almost 40 ft. high, 3 ft. in diameter, and shone like silver in the morning sunshine. "Fly," murmured Dr. Walter Ziegler. The German engineer pressed a red button in his safety shelter. An enormous jet of flame shot out of the lower end of the shining object. Leaving the ground slowly it gradually increased in speed until it was only a speck in the blue sky. This took place on the morning of March 1, 1981. The scene of action was a small oasis in the Sahara Desert about 500 miles south of Tripoli, Libya's capital. The "object" was a rocket built by the Orbital Transport and Rocket Co. Ltd. in Germany. OTRAG has always maintained that they were building rockets solely for peaceful purposes. But since this test in the desert, it is obvious that OTRAG is making military rockets for Libya.

This trial missile traveled merely 180 miles.

Nevertheless, Libya's fanatic Chief of State, Muammar el-Gadhafi, wants more: Middle and long-distance rockets which can carry ton-loads of bombs and travel over 4,000 miles. Rockets made on their own oil-rich desert land but manufactured by German technicians. This "Madman of Tripoli" (as called by the *London Observer*) is willing to go to any cost. He has set aside $1.5 billion for a five-year program. Added to this, Libya and the OTRAG have drawn up a secret contract which was signed in Zurich, Switzerland in January, 1980.

In actual fact, this is all part of a fightful plan. Gadhafi, whose only dream is a great Islamic State and the destruction of Israel, made the agreement with OTRAG on one condition. This condition was mentioned by a high Libyan government official: "OTRAG has promised to supply us with rockets which can carry nuclear warheads."

There is no wonder that such things are happening TODAY! No one expects or speaks about it. One thing is certain though: Libya will be in the front lines of the war when Meshech and Tubal march against Israel.

Israel's successful attack on Iraq's nuclear plant was not the end of Israel's troubles. They are even increasing. Today's situation in Israel was described hundreds of years ago by the prophets, for instance in Isaiah 66:8, *"Who hath heard such a thing? Who hath seen such things? Shall the earth be made to bring forth in one day? Or shall a nation be born at once? For as soon as Zion travailed, she brought forth her children."* All of these threats on Israel are birthpains which must precede her spiritual restoration. It is a known fact in Israel that the Messianic era will be introduced by all kinds of tribulation, i.e., natural catastrophes, a spread of godlessness and immorality, militant attacks by godless powers on Jerusalem and the Jewish people who have returned home. According

Gadhafi, a fanatic Moslem, is solidly united with Communism when it comes to oppose Israel.

to one Orthodox Jew, "These are the footsteps of the Messiah." In the Talmud it is written, "War against Israel signifies the beginning of our redemption."

My brethren, this is true for us also; surely you sense how war — trials and tribulations — in the invisible world is increasing, but this is the beginning of our salvation. For *"The morning cometh, and also the night,"* (Isaiah 21:12). Our Lord is coming!

The whole of nature is waiting for us to be revealed as God's children. *"For the earnest*

The most modern and sophisticated Russian missles are in the hands of Lybia's dictator, Gadhafi. Libya has become one of Israel's gravest threats.

expectation of the creature waiteth for the manifestation of the sons of God. For the creature was made subject to vanity, not willingly, but by reason of him who hath subjected the same in hope, because the creature itself also shall be delivered from the bondage of corruption into the glorious liberty of the children of God. For we know that the whole creation groaneth and travaileth in pain together until now. And not only they, but ourselves also, which have the first fruits of the Spirit, even we ourselves groan within ourselves waiting for the adoption, to wit, the redemption of our body, (Romans 8:19-23). The wonderful promise is that *creation* will also be renewed after we have been raptured and the marriage feast of the Lamb has begun, and after we have returned with the Lord in power and great glory to the Mount of Olives for the millennium. Everything will be renewed during this indescribable thousand-year reign of peace.

The more Israel is threatened the more she longs for peace. In the same way, the more we are troubled on every side the more we long for the Lord to come!

Israel realizes the danger she is in, that can

be concluded from the continuation of the following report:

> For the purpose of short, medium and long distance rocket-deterrent as well as for Air Defense, a total of 1,943 rockets should be produced by those firms who are participating in the Delta Project in Saudi-Arabia, etc. But nothing became of the arrangement! The discrete oil sheiks found out that the 'strictly confidential' Delta Plan had landed in the hands of the Israel secret service, Mossad."

But this forceful advance of Libya, especially after the destruction of Iraq's atomic center confirms that the day is very near.

> Gadhafi is wild with anger and what particularly aggravates him is that not only American airplanes and equipment were used for the raid, but also the renowned American AWAC's surveillance system completely failed. The Israeli aircraft did return home safely. The safety installation provided for by Western Europe for the Osirak installation did not even permit an attempt of a defensive action against Israel.
>
> Gadhafi himself has submitted a secret plan to the leading Arab Petro-Dollar potentates; a nuclear armament fund for the production of an Islamic-Arab atom bomb. The installation is to be set up outside the range of Israeli or American reach. At a conference in Baghdad of Arab Petro-Dollar potentates no agreement was reached on

Petro dollars have brought much wealth to Libya, part of which is used to support terror groups, such as PLO, generously.

Newsweek Magazine sees Gadhafi as the most dangerous man in the world.

Gadhafi's project, but it was decided first of all to send a delegation to Islamabad and Moscow to determine further action on the grounds of expert opinion from Pakistan."

In this way, Meshech and Tubal are being compelled by their vassals to move forward in their battle against Israel. We must not have any illusions about Libya's neighboring land, Egypt, either. Although Egypt is today at enmity with Libya, despite all her former peace declarations, she has exactly the same secret aim as Libya and all the other enemies of Israel, for it has been made known that,

Egypt's ex-President, the late Anwar Sadat, sent a note (in his own handwriting) to the League of Arab Islamic Peoples in Tunis appealing for 'the liberation of Jerusalem' and that the Palestinians should have 'an eternal, national and religious right to Jerusalem,' and that from now on May 30th (Israeli conquest of Jerusalem) should be celebrated as 'the international day for an Arab Jerusalem.'

Ethiopia

Ethiopia, formerly called Abyssinia, has also come into the spotlight of prophecy. It is specifically named in Ezekiel 38:5 (see introductory Bible verses). Together with Persia and Libya, Ethiopia will be part of the

Ben Baruch is working desparately to help save the Jews of Ethiopia.

Russian train in the war against Israel.

Geographically, Ethiopia lies south of Egypt with Sudan in between. Ethiopia is one of the world's poorest countries. Her 28 million inhabitants, mostly farmers, are from about thirty different ethnical groups; they are a mixture of Ham's descendants and Arab immigrants who crossed the Red Sea in the Middle Ages. The Hebrew word for Ethiopia is "Cush" and means not only "dark colored" or "black" but also "a collection of peoples." This shows that Ethiopia is a people of no clear identity. It is a fatal mixture of Jewry, Islam, and Christianity, which practices not only the Jewish circumcision but also Christian baptism. It is interesting to note that the last Emperor, Haili Selassie called himself, "The lion of Judah."

Today Ethiopia is in league with Moscow and has therefore a dimension which is missing in Libya; namely, Communism. But

Ethiopia, one of the poorest countries in the world. Picture shows workers harvesting sugar cane by hand.

as neither Ethiopia nor Libya have any particular role in God's plan of salvation for the world, their origins cannot be traced back like Israel's, which is very clearly named in the Bible. Nevertheless, this land, Ethiopia, is a danger to Israel because it is named as such in Ezekiel 38 and because it has already

Queen Sheba of Ethiopia visited King Solomon of Israel.

become Russianized.

While Ethiopia is being ideologically infected by Communism, Libya — being fanatically Moslem — is only being influenced by Communism militarily. In a Communist booklet we read, "Our main aim in the Ethiopian revolution is to foster political consciousness and found a workers' party!"

Looking back at Ethiopia's history we can see quite a few interesting points. Although the spreading of the Gospel was cut off by Islam in the 7th century, she still remained true to her root. It is rather interesting to see that this country was touched by the Lord in both the New Testament and the Old Testament. In the Old Testament it was the Ethiopian Queen of Sheba who came and saw Solomon's glory and said, *"Behold, the half was not told me,"* (I Kings 10:7). Through King Solomon she came in contact with the law of God and the Psalms. The Word of God was spread throughout her country as a result.

In the New Testament we read that shortly after Pentecost, the message of the Lamb of God was carried by the Ethiopian Eunuch back to his land and to Candace, the queen. *"And the angel of the Lord spake unto Philip, saying, Arise, and go toward the south unto the way that goeth down from Jerusalem unto Gaza, which is desert. And he arose and went: and, behold, a man of Ethiopia, an eunuch of great authority under Candace queen of the Ethiopians, who had the charge of all her treasure, and had come to Jerusalem for to worship, was returning, and sitting in his chariot read Esaias the prophet. Then the Spirit said unto Philip, Go near, and join thyself to this chariot. And Philip ran thither to him, and heard him read the prophet Esaias, and said, Understandest thou what thou readest? And he said, How can I, except some man should guide me? And he desired Philip that he would come up and sit with him. The place of the Scripture which he read was this, He was led as a sheep to the slaughter; and like a lamb dumb before his shearer, so opened he not his mouth: In his humiliation his judgment was taken away: and who shall declare his generation? for his life is taken from the earth. And the eunuch answered Philip, and said, I pray thee, of whom speaketh the prophet this? of himself, or of some other man? Then Phillip opened his mouth, and began at the same Scripture, and preached unto him Jesus. And as they went on their way,*

Ethiopia's emperor lost control of his country to the Communists has in the meantime died.

*they came unto a certain water: and the eunuch
said, See, here is water; what doth hinder me to
be baptized? And Philip said, If thou believest
with all thine heart, thou mayest. And he
answered and said, I believe that Jesus Christ
is the Son of God. And he commanded the
chariot to stand still; and they went down both
into the water, both Philip and the eunuch; and
he baptized him. And when they were come up
out of the water, the Spirit of the Lord caught
away Philip, that the eunuch saw him no more:
and he went on his way rejoicing,"* (Acts 8:26-
39).

The Word of God therefore came to Ethiopia
from Jerusalem. But Ethiopia will end up
with the bands who will come upon Israel like
a stormcloud (Ezekiel 38:9, 16).

Ezekiel 38:6 mentions two other nations
other than Ethiopia and Libya, who will
come against Israel in the latter days;
namely, Gomer and Togarmah, *"Gomer, and
all his bands; the house of Togarmah of the
north quarters, and all his bands: and many
people with thee."*

Gomer

In the Talmud, Gomer is also translated
"Germany." Genesis 10:3 tells us their origin,

"And the sons of Gomer; Ashkenaz, and Riphath, and Togarmah." From history we learn that these three sons of Gomer moved from Asia Minor to the north coast of the Black Sea. The area was called "Gomeria," later "Cimeria," and later still "Crimea." The families of Riphath and Togarmah settled

In spite of poor economy, Ethiopia is arming itself. Boys as young as twelve years of age are in the military service. The uniforms are red.

around the Black Sea while the other descendants of Gomer — Ashkenaz — moved north-
ward along the river Danube inhabiting
present-day Germany, at first called Gomer-
land and later Germania. Strangely enough,
German-speaking Jews even today are called
Ashkenazim" which is the plural form of the
descendants of Ashkenaz. This does not mean
to say that all of Gomer's descendants are to
be found in Germany, but Ezekiel 38:6 does
refer to at least part of the German nation.

This prophecy, spoken 2,500 years ago,
says that this will all take place in the LATTER
YEARS and that is today, *"After many days
thou shalt be visited: in the latter years thou
shalt come into the land that is brought back
from the sword, and is gathered out of many
people, against the mountains of Israel, which
have been always waste: but it is brought forth
out of the nations, and they shall dwell safely
all of them."*

Germany helped in a most cruel way to
expel and destroy the Jews from Europe. God
will therefore lead Germany, under the
leadership of Russia, to the land of the Jews
where He will settle account with her.

These details are of considerable signifi-
cance in connection with Russia's aims and

The soldiers of Gomer (East Germany) will march with the Soviet Union against Israel.

associations in these last times. Based on these facts, those who have studied the prophetic Word centuries ago already declared that Germany and Russia would join together. The hostile attitude of the Nazi regime toward Bolshevism made such a development appear impossible at that time. Today, however, the German Democratic Republic (East Germany) is Russia's closest friend and simultaneously the Soviet's elongated arm, from which we can already see the final outcome!

God's Word is the Truth and He has the last word, also as far as your personal life is concerned; therefore put your whole trust in Him, for He says that those who put their trust in Him will never be put to shame.

Togarmah

Togarmah is named in the same sentence as Gomer, and lies not only in the north but in *"the uttermost parts of the north"* (Ezekiel 38:6 Amplified Bible). Togarmah lies so far north that between her and Israel lie Lebanon and Syria. This land is today's Turkey.

Sensational things are also happening in Turkey; both the Soviet Union (Asia) and the NATO (the West) are trying to claim Turkey.

Turkey, too, will have to follow the footsteps of Russia, according to the Prophet Ezekiel.

But Russia will win. The way for it was being paved during the Cyprus crisis several years ago. "Greece, Turkey's neighbor, will join with United Europe, i.e., the Roman empire, while Turkey, despite her dictatorship, will join Asia," as we stated long ago. Turkey, who is becoming increasingly anti-Israel is predestined to join Russia's train against Israel.

All these things are now in full swing. To you who are reading these lines, I say again, *"Seek ye out of the book of the Lord, and read: no one of these shall fail, none shall want her mate: for my mouth it hath commanded, and his spirit it hath gathered them. And he hath cast the lot for them, and his hand hath divided it unto them by line: they shall possess it for ever, from generation to generation shall they dwell therein"* (Isaiah 34:16-17).

Today ask the Lord to cleanse you and prepare you, for He is coming soon!

Chapter 3

Jordan, Saudi Arabia, and Iraq in Bible Prophecy

"When the most High divided to the nations · their inheritance, when he separated the sons of Adam, he set the bounds of the people according to the number of the children of Israel" (Deuteronomy 32:8).

"By myself have I sworn, saith the Lord, for because thou hast done this thing, and hast not withheld thy son, thine only son: that in blessing I will bless thee, and in multiplying I will multiply thy seed as the stars of the heaven, and as the sand which is upon the sea shore; and thy seed shall possess the gate of his enemies" (Genesis 22:16-17).

Deuteronomy 28:13 shows that the nations' borders are entirely determined by and dependent on Israel.

Genesis 22:16-17 describes the seed of Abraham as being like the stars of heaven and like the sand on the sea shore. Abraham is the father of all who believe and the stars therefore represent the heavenly people of God, the Church of Jesus Christ. The sand on the sea shore represents the earthly people of God, Israel. Just as the sand regulates the ocean, so Israel regulates the sea of nations.

We are now going to consider three of the nations that lie around Israel whose enmity toward Israel has been obvious since 1948. Before May of that year, all of these three countries were dormant, but the moment Israel's resurrection began, it seems as though the spirits of the surrounding nations were also revived. Whenever other nations are mentioned in the Bible, it is always in connection with Israel because Israel is the nucleus of all God's actions. Ezekiel 5:5 says, *"Thus saith the Lord God; This is Jerusalem: I have set it in the midst of the nations and countries that are round about her."* Biblically speaking, therefore, Israel is the center of the world and Jerusalem is the center of Israel. It is only to be expected, then, that the spirit and attitude of these surrounding peoples are being drawn into and affected by today's quick succession of fulfilled prophecies. This means that the attitude of all nations, and not only that of Jordan, Saudi Arabia and Iraq,

Sultan Kabus Oman, an early ruler bordering Saudi Arabia.

whether voluntarily or involuntarily, will be revealed in confrontation with Israel. The very nature of every nation will be disclosed when faced with Israel. It will then be

Today's King Hussein of Jordan.

obvious and apparent to which spirit each belongs. The reappearing of Israel is proof to the truth of God's Word. God is giving this to us because we are now in the interim period between believing and seeing. When God begins to give proof, it shows that the end must be near because He does not normally give proof; He wants us to believe and live by faith.

Zechariah 8:3 calls Jerusalem the *"city of truth."* Truth always unites with truth, whereas truth and lies always oppose one another. The Lord Jesus said in Luke 17:1, *"It is impossible but that offences will come: but woe unto him, through whom they come!"* In our own life as believers, too, if we walk in the light our experience will be similar to Israel's. Objectively speaking, Israel is called "elect and beloved for the forefathers' sakes." She is continually in conflicts because she is an object of truth on this earth. All conflicts in our personal lives, whether inward or outward, are always caused by the collision of truth and lies. Therefore it is very important to ask ourselves: Am I standing and walking completely in the truth? Am I in Jesus Christ? If the answer is positive, the conflict and the adversaries you experience are from outside — through people who misjudge or attack you. But if you live untruthfully, if you are half for the Lord and half for the world, then your life is not light, but darkness. It is not ordered aright and cleansed through the blood of Jesus. Your testimony is a lie. In this case, the conflict is within you. In the same way, Israel has both internal and external conflicts today.

Jordan

This is a relatively new state. Before World War II, it was called Trans-Jordan, and previous to that it belonged to Arabia. Its capital is Amman, which originally belonged to the children of Ammon. Moab was Ammon's neighbor in the south. Today both these districts belong to Jordan. These two antique peoples, whose names are no longer used, (Ammonites and Moabites) descended from the two sons of Lot, Ammon and Moab. At the time when Lot was saved from Sodom, through the prayers of his uncle Abraham, and was literally dragged out, at the hands of angels, he went to live in a cave; the result of this was an incestuous relationship with his two daughters, thus Moab and Ammon were born who became a thorn in Israel's side from then onwards.

This brings us to the root of Jordan's trouble; it is her attitude of wanting the best of both worlds. The Jordanian king, Hussein, has negotiated with all of the various Israeli statesmen — Golda Meir, Eshcol, Perez, and the late Moshe Dayan — but at the same time his relationship with Israel's enemies is also positive. This attitude can be traced back to Lot, his ancestor. Lot was the son of Abraham's deceased brother, Nahor, and always appeared to be undecided, without a clear personal spiritual identity. Nothing is worse in Christian discipleship than to "halt between two opinions" — for Christ and for the world — like Lot was, and like Hussein still is today. What is the result of being hot and cold? Jesus calls it "Lukewarm" in Revelation 3:16.

The first time Lot comes onto the scene is in Genesis 12:4. The Lord had called Abraham, in Genesis 12:1-4, *"Get thee out of thy country, and from thy kindred, and from thy father's house, unto a land that I will shew thee: and I will make of thee a great nation, and I will bless thee, and make thy name great; and thou shalt be a blessing; and I will bless them that bless thee, and curse him that curseth thee: and in thee shall all families of the earth be blessed. So Abraham departed, as the Lord had spoken unto him..."* There should be a period there

Israeli border police at watch.

but there is a comma instead, *"...and Lot went with him."* Lot was not obeying a call, he just went along with Abraham. We do not know Abraham's motives for taking Lot either. If he had not taken him, there would have been no Ammonites and Moabites, and therefore no Jordan, today. One of Abraham's motives could have been that if he and his beloved and beautiful wife, Sarah, did not receive a baby they could use Lot as their heir instead. But it soon became clear, in Genesis 13, that the land could not bear both Lot and Abraham, because they both had so many cattle and the herdsmen of the one were continually quarreling with the other's, so they had to part company. After they separated the Lord spoke once again to Abraham. Lot's company was disastrous for Abraham, but for Lot himself it was revealing; it exposed the real motives of his heart. For instance, when the Lord wanted to save Lot from destruction together with Sodom, because of Abraham's prayers for him, Lot wavered and lingered. That was his character, a continual procrastinator and hesitator. Genesis 19:17-19 reads, *"And it came to pass, when they had brought them forth abroad, that he said, Escape for thy life; look not behind thee, neither stay thou in all the plain; escape to the mountain, lest thou be consumed. And Lot said unto them, OH, NOT SO, MY LORD."* That is the sort of person who always says "Yes" and "No" to the Lord, and never gives an unconditional "Yes." This is what causes inner confusion and strife in your walk with God. The result of wavering and wanting the best of both worlds, in Lot's case, was a disgraceful end. I am most troubled when I think of those among my readers who linger undecidedly without an unconditional "Yes" to the Lord and "No" to sin. Listen! Destruction has already set in, so make haste and save your soul! *"Work out your own salvation with fear and trembling"* (Philippians 2:12b). Jesus is waiting for you.

As we have already said, King Hussein who lives in Amman also wants the best of both worlds; but because of his halting between two opinions, he lost possession of Israel's most holy places in 1967 — the Wailing Wall and Temple Square — when they fell into Israeli hands. Needless to say, he had desecrated and profaned this holy ground during the time of Jordanian rule. They even had built public facilities using stones from the prophets' tombs. It is strange how people all over the world always protest against Israel's actions but nobody protested against that desecration! In this way Jordan, the two brothers Moab and Ammon, mocked and despised Israel, and the prophecy of Ezekiel 25:1-7 is coming to pass, *"The Word of the Lord came again unto me saying, Son of man, set thy face against the Ammonites, and prophesy against them; And say unto the Ammonites, Hear the Word of the Lord God; Thus saith the Lord God; Because thou saidst, Aha, against my sanctuary, when it was profaned; and against the land of Israel, when it was desolate; and against the house of Judah, when they went into captivity: Behold, Therefore I will deliver thee to the men of the east for a possession, and they shall set their palaces in thee, and make their dwellings in thee: they shall eat thy fruit, and they shall drink thy milk, and I will make Rabbah* (that is present day Amman) *a stable for camels, and the Ammonites a couching place for flocks: and ye shall know that I am the Lord. For thus saith the Lord God; because thou hast clapped thine hands, and stamped with thy feet, and rejoiced in heart with all thy despite against the land of Israel; behold, therefore I will stretch out mine hand upon thee, and will deliver thee for a spoil to the heathen; and I will cut thee off from the people, and I will cause thee to perish out of the countries: I will destroy thee: and thou shalt know that I am the Lord."*

That is the judgment on Jordan. The rest of her judgment is described as God continues to speak about Moab, in verse 8, *"Thus saith the Lord God; Because that Moab and Seir do say, Behold, the house of Judah is like unto all the heathen* (in other words, Why do you say Israel is a chosen nation?). *Therefore, Behold, I will open the side of Moab from the cities, from his cities, which are on his frontiers, the glory of the country, Beth-Jeshimoth, Baal-Meon, and Kiriathaim, unto the men of the east with the Ammonites, and will give them in possession, that the Ammonites may not be remembered among the nations. And I will execute judgments upon Moab; and they shall know that I am the Lord."* My friends, this will be fulfilled because they were pleased about Israel's suffering and troubles and because they have desecrated Israel's sanctuary. These are all the by-products of a divided heart! If your heart is divided toward the

Lord Jesus Christ you will take undefinable malicious pleasure in the trials of those who follow the Lord with all of their hearts. You will mix the holy with the unholy things in your daily life, like Jordan is doing even to this day.

Saudi Arabia

This is the richest country in the world and a concentrated enemy of Israel. Almost the whole world bows down to her because of her oil. The Arabian Peninsula is the whole territory of Saudi Arabia, North and South Yemen and the Gulf Emirates, whose peoples were originally nomads — and some still are today — being the descendants of Ishmael, Medan, Midian and Jokshan. All of these were direct descendants of Abraham.

Ishmael, the ruling factor among the Arabs, was the first-fruit of Abraham's impatience. In Genesis 16 we read that Abraham could no longer wait for God to fulfill His promise to give him and Sarah a son, and he listened to the female logic of his wife to take her Egyptian servant, Hagar, as a second wife and so perhaps get the promised son. In this way they thought they

audi Arabia's
heik Yamani

could help God to answer their prayer! They are not the only ones, for I have often seen people "help God to fulfill His Word"! I am sure that Abraham was very proud of his boy Ishmael and said, "Thank you Lord for this child!" But God told him that Ishmael was not the heir, not the son He had promised to Sarah. What trials came with Ishmael, even to our present day!

Medan, Midian and Jokshan were the sons of Keturah whom Abraham married after he had received the promised son, Isaac, and after Sarah had died. These were all fleshly sons and not sons of the promise. The whole family of Keturah increased just like the family of Ishmael. They inter-married and became the greatest hazard for Israel for thousands of years. As a young nation, Israel's hardest battles were against the Midianites. In Judges 6:3-4 we read, *"And so it was, when Israel had sown, that the Midianites came up, and the Amalekites, and the children of the east...and they destroyed the increase of the earth, till thou come unto Gaza, and left no sustenance for Israel, neither sheep, nor ox, nor ass."*

Nehemiah 2:17-19 also refers to the enmity

◄ Saudi Arabia's sheik Yamani has a powerful grip on the U.S.A.

of the Arabs and Ammon, too. *"Then said I unto them, Ye see the distress that we are in, how Jerusalem lieth waste, and the gates thereof are burned with fire: come, and let us build up the wall of Jerusalem, that we be no more a reproach. Then I told them of a reproach. Then I told them of the hand of my God which was good upon me; as also the king's words that he had spoken unto me. And they said, Let us rise up and build. So they strengthened their hands for this good work. But when Sanballat the Horonite, and Tobiah the servant, the AMMONITE and Geshem, the ARABIAN, heard it, they laughed us to scorn, and despised us, and said, What is this thing that ye do? Will ye rebel against the king?"*

As long as Jerusalem lay in ruins nobody bothered about it, but as soon as the Jews returned it was instantly difficult! The Arabs and Ammonites in Nehemiah's day were furious when they saw that the Jews were serious about making Jerusalem their eternal capital, *"But it came to pass that when Sanballat, and Tobiah, and the Arabians, and the Ammonites, and the Ashodites* (the Gaza Strip), *heard that the walls of Jerusalem were made up, and that the breaches began to be*

*stopped, then they were very wroth, and con-
sidered all of them together to come and to fight
against Jerusalem, and to hinder it. Nevertheless we made our prayer unto our God, and set
a watch against them day and night, because of
them"* (Nehemiah 4:7-9). That all sounds very
modern. Although the Arabs already then
were at variance with one another yet they
became *united* in an alliance against Jerusalem. There is nothing new under the sun!
Today, too, Saudi Arabia together with
Jordan are furious because Jerusalem is
being rebuilt under Israeli sovreignty. They
have declared a "holy war" against Israel as
have also the other Arabs, who are not a
single nation but just a group of peoples
without any clear identity, and are a perilous
danger to Israel.

I want to give you a word of warning here:
Just as this mixture of peoples with no clear
identity came about through unbelief and
disobedience on the part of Israel's patri-
archs has increased mightily by their continually laying claim to the land which God has
promised to Israel with the world's full
approval, so every sin of unbelief and
disobedience in my life and yours, which we

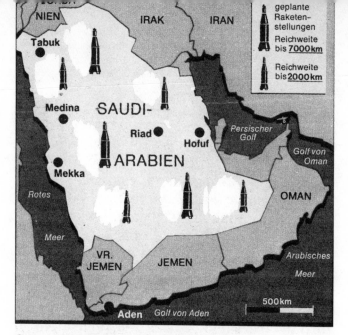

German masterplan for missle system in Saudi Arabia.

refuse to give up and therefore remains
unforgiven, darkens our spiritual identity,
wiping out the light of the glorious Gospel of
Christ in us. This is the enemy's sole aim for
you and for Israel, to wipe out and destroy our
identity, our election, that which makes us
special. The U.N. also puts Israel on a par
with all the other nations saying, "Judah is
the same *as all the other Gentiles.*" Psalm
83:3-4 is a forthright description of their
attitude, *"They have taken crafty counsel
against thy people, and consulted against thy
hidden ones. They have said, Come, and let us
cut them off from being a nation; that the name*

of Israel may be no more in remembrance." This is what they are still striving for today. My Brother and Sister, the enemy's intended goal in your life is that you lose your identity so that Christ is no longer seen in you. Don't you feel how he wants to rob you of what is yours, the gifts you have from the Lord and in the Lord? The Scriptures warn us of this, *"Behold, I come quickly: hold that fast which thou hast, that no man take thy crown"* (Revelation 3:11). Ephesians 6:13 has newly impressed me in this connection, *"Wherefore take unto you the whole armour of God, that ye may be able to withstand in the evil day* (and surely this is an evil day, especially for Israel) *and having done all, to stand."* Israel certainly has to watch day and night also against Saudi Arabia, who is being armed to its teeth by all the Western countries including the United States of America.

Saudi Arabia is a rich country — who knows how rich! — and although she has a dislike for Russia at present, when the time coems she will encourage and agree with the hordes who will come from the north to attack Israel. Ezekiel 38:9-13 says, *"Thou shalt ascend and come like a storm, thou shalt be like a cloud to cover the land, thou, and all thy bands, and many people with thee. Thus saith the Lord God; It shall also come to pass, that at the same time shall things come into thy mind, and thou shalt think an evil thought: and thou shalt say, I will go up to the land of unwalled villages; I will go to them that are at rest, that dwell safely, all of them dwelling without walls, and having neither bars nor gates, to take a spoil, and to take a prey; to turn thine hand upon the desolate places that are now inhabited, and upon the people that are gathered out of the nations* (Israel), *that have gotten cattle and goods, that dwell in the midst of the land. Sheba* (German Bible says "Rich Arabia" instead of Sheba) *and Dedan and the merchants of Tarshish, with all the young lions thereof, shall say unto thee, Art thou come to take a spoil?..."*

Those of you who read your Bibles carefully will think that the first verses of Ezekiel 38, where it speaks of the prince of Meshech and Tubal coming and covering the land of Israel like a storm cloud, can surely only be fulfilled when Israel is dwelling safely without walls or gates, which is certainly not the case yet. You are quite right. Yet this is what is happening through the crisis in Lebanon; Israel's nothern border is opening increasingly and that is the direction from where disaster is to come. We must look at the crisis in Lebanon from a Biblical point of view.

Lebanon is the battleground where Syria and Israel are confronting one another. The Lord says that Israel is going to be freed of these thorns on her borders soon! Speaking directly to Tyre and Sidon, Lebanon's leading cities, the Lord says in Ezekiel 28:20-26, *"Again the Word of the Lord came unto me, saying, Son of man, set thy face against Zidon, and prophesy against it, and say Thus saith the Lord God: Behold, I am against thee, O Zidon: and I will be glorified in the midst of thee: and they shall know that I am the Lord, when I shall have executed judgments in her, and shall be sanctified in her. For I will send into her pestilence, and blood into her streets; and the wounded shall be judged in the midst of her by the sword upon her on every side; and they shall know that I am the Lord."*

Surely this is what we are seeing today. Then comes the reason, *"And there shall be no more a pricking brier unto the house of Israel, nor any grieving thorn of all that are round*

*about them, that despised them; and they shall
know that I am the Lord God. Thus saith the
Lord God; When I shall have gathered the
house of Israel from the people among whom
they are scattered, and shall be sanctified in
them in the sight of the heathen, then shall they
dwell in their land that I have given to my
servant Jacob. And they shall* DWELL SAFELY
*therein, and shall build houses, and plant
vineyards; yea, they shall dwell with confi-
dence, when I have executed judgments upon
all those that despise them round about them;
and they shall know that I am the Lord their
God."* This is the outcome of the Lebanon
crisis. It must come to an explosion because
Lebanon is on the direct route from the Soviet
Union to Israel. According to our under-
standing of the Scripture, hostilities can
break out overnight; it is in the balance. But
the final result will be peace in the north.

Iraq

Although Iraq lies about 650 miles from
Israel, she is one of Israel's most ferocious
enemies. Historically speaking, Iraq is the
result of a mixture of Biblical events. Para-
dise was in Iraq. It was there that Satan first

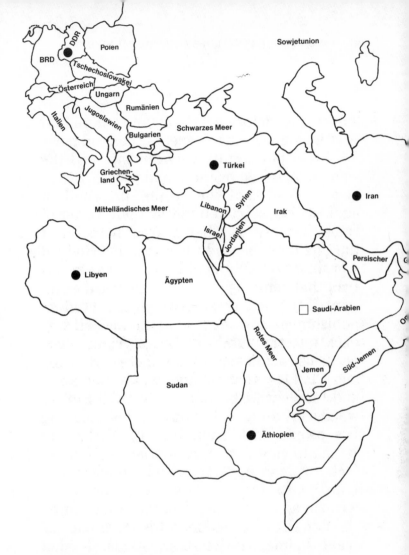

- Countries under Russian influence.
- □ Saudi Arabia encouraging Soviet invasion of Israel.

Note Israel's size in comparison with the Arab world (compare Isaiah 41:14).

gained the victory over man and where God first announced the Gospel — the good news — "I will put enmity between thee and the woman, between her seed and yours." It was also in Iraq that the people, in rebellion against God, started building their Tower of Babel (Genesis 11). It was from here, Ur of the Chaldees, beyond the river, that God led Abraham to the land of Israel. It was to this Iraq that centuries later Abraham's descendants (the ten tribes) were deported as punishment for their idolatry and sins — back into the hands of the Assyrians, their previous enemies. It was also here in Babylon and Chaldea, that the two tribes, Benjamin and Judah, were brought as captives. But the wonderful thing is that God has been leading His people back from Iraq to the land of Israel. In view of all these national-historical facts, we can understand why particularly Iraq wants to manufacture the deadliest weapon against Israel, i.e., the atom bomb.

After the destruction of the Iraqi nuclear plant, Prime Minister Begin explained that they had been compelled to act instantaneously because they knew that ultimately the Iraqis meant to make atom bombs which

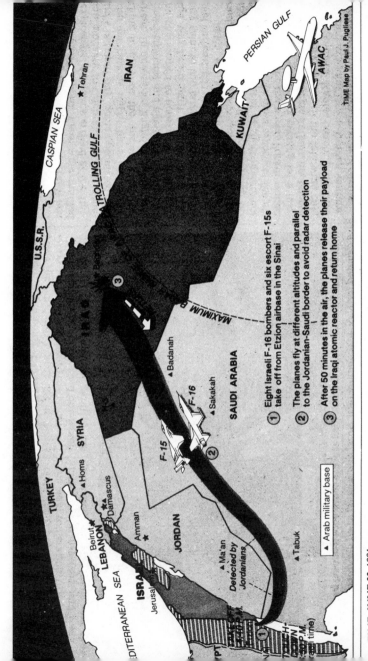

PERSIAN GULF

IRAN

CASPIAN SEA

U.S.S.R.

★ Tehran

AWAC

KUWAIT

TROLLING GULF

MAXIMUM B

IRAQ

③

▲ Badanah

SAUDI ARABIA

▲ Sakakah

F-16

F-15

②

TURKEY

SYRIA

▲ Homs

Beirut ★
LEBANON ★★ Damascus

JORDAN

★ Amman

▲ Ma'an

Detected by
Jordanians

▲ Tabuk

ISRAEL

Jerusalem

MEDITERRANEAN SEA

①

① Eight Israeli F-16 bombers and six escort F-15s
take off from Etzion airbase in the Sinai

② The planes fly at different altitudes and parallel
to the Jordanian-Saudi border to avoid radar detection

③ After 50 minutes in the air, the planes release their payload
on the Iraqi atomic reactor and return home

▲ Arab military base

TIME Map by Paul J. Pugliese

TIME, JUNE 22, 1981

were intended for the destruction of Israel. For instance, in an Iraqi newspaper, *El Taura* October 4, 1980 Saddam Hussein, the President of Iraq, was quoted as saying to Iran, "You do not need to fear our nuclear plant, it is intended for Israel!" Iran had tried to bomb this plant the previous September but had failed. This statement was only one of many coming from Baghdad which made their intentions quite clear. Begin said that three twenty-ton bombs would kill 600,000 and the survival of his whole nation would be jeopardized. Even though most of the world is crying out that Iraq was only carrying out nuclear research for peaceful purposes, America knows better — although our government nevertheless criticized Israel's action. In March, 1981 the Democratic Senator, Alan Cranstone of California, published in a protocol the facts he knew about the Iraqi research plant. He said that it had been confirmed to him by government officials that Iraq had bought large supplies of uranium in Portugal and that she and Brazil had pooled their knowledge concerning nuclear energy; furthermore, Iraq had made an agreement with France in the key areas of nuclear technology apart from the nuclear reactors, including the necessary highly concentrated fuel suitable for nuclear arms which France has sold to Iraq. He said that Italy has supplied Iraq with the necessary means of extracting plutonium from the

Iraq's special anti-aircraft units (Russian made) were ineffective against Israel's lightening raid.

nuclear reactors bought from France and that both France and Italy are training several hundred specialists in a program for highly sensitive nuclear technology in Iraq. In fact, the Iraqis are undertaking everything possible in order to possess nuclear technology, thus enabling them to build nuclear explosives. And all of these activities are being carried out in return for Iraq's oil!

For the first time in these forty years of nuclear history, nuclear technology has been used to destroy a nuclear reactor in a military attack. Forty is often used in the Bible as a time of testing. For instance, Israel's forty years in the wilderness and Jesus' forty days of testing by the devil. There are many forties mentioned in the Bible. The fact that after forty years of nuclear history, it is Zion, Jerusalem, who deals such a blow, is certainly prophetic. It warns us that the danger of a nuclear catastrophe has come frighteningly near for this world. Israel's action was like a command from above to halt and restrain the devil's compulsion to destroy. Joel 3:16 says, *"The Lord also shall roar out of Zion, and utter his voice from Jerusalem; and the heavens and the earth shall shake: but the Lord will be the hope of his people, and the strength of the children of Israel."* People who pass judgment on Israel so superficially are very short-sighted.

The great Israeli prophet Daniel also held up destruction in Babel — present day Iraq — although it was not by an atom bomb at that time. King Nebuchadnezar commanded that all his wise men, magicians, astrologers and sorcerers be put to death because they could not tell him the dream he had had and its meaning! When Arioch, the captain of the king's guard, came to Daniel, Daniel said, "Stop! God in heaven knows everything! Tell the king to wait...!" Daniel held up the threat of death for everyone. The spiritual application for us is that we must be such who hold up the wave of spiritual destruction which is at present flooding over us, wherever we live. How are we to do this? By complete obedience in faith! Copy what Israel did in Iraq: hit the enemy where he needs to be hit. Strike the enemy with the victory of Jesus at the very place where HE will otherwise destroy you. The enemy's work in your life must be struck at the point he attacks you.

It is also revealing for us, who have to fight

the good fight of faith to see HOW Israel carried out this operation, for I Corinthians 10:6 tells us that Israel is our example.

Israel had to hit her goal in a matter of minutes before the radar-controlled Air Defense of Baghdad could intervene. This precision work had been practiced for months on a model in the desert. It was not only a matter of hitting the reactor but of calculating the degree of approach in such a way that the bombs would not rebound and explode harmlessly in the air, but penetrate the concrete-clad reactor exploding shortly afterwards. The Israelis used their self-made 2,000 lb. Paveway laser-guided bombs which are carried by the F-16s. The most critical part of the whole operation was the timing. It was not by chance that the six Israeli F-15s and F-16s appeared over Tamuz, 15 miles from Baghdad, at 6:35 p.m. local time. It was just at night fall, and light enough to hit the target and then fly off and disappear into the coming darkness. Night falls within minutes in the Orient.

The raid was also timed so that none of the French technicians would be at the site, being after closing hours. Moreover it was

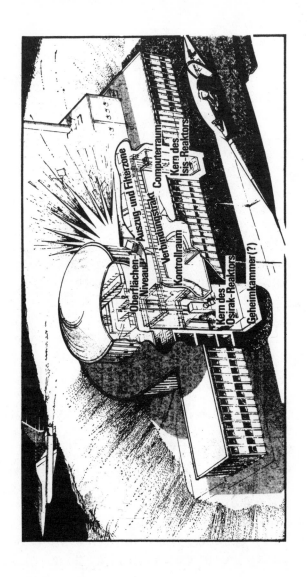

The timing was perfect, the destruction total.

Pentecost Sunday and a public holiday for the "Christian" workers — thus providing a double safeguard.

A French technician, employed by a French building firm in Tamuz, observed the raid from the terrace of a restaurant and gave his eye-witness account on arriving back in Paris. He said that he had seen four military aircraft fly twice over the plant dropping four bombs; the accuracy of the bombardment was incredible. The central building and reactor were instantly destroyed and it was all over in two minutes. He further said that if Iraq intended carrying on work there, it would be necessary to start from scratch. He had the impression that the whole operation had hit the intended goal within an inch!

Why am I quoting all these details which you have probably read anyway in your newspapers? It is so that we learn from Israel, and fight the good fight of faith with similar accuracy and precision. II Timothy 2:5 says, *"And if a man also strive for masteries, yet is he not crowned, except he strive lawfully."* Each of us must fight the fight of faith in God's way. I often have the impression that we do not make use of the victory of Jesus effectively but squander His unlimited power to overcome the enemy of our soul by using it for our own edification. We may make lots of religious noise but the old enemy is left untouched as far as our family or church is concerned.

American satellite photos proved the French technicians' words true: each bomb hit the intended target. Israel made its destructive attack on the enemy's center of danger and succeeded. When I saw the spiritual application of this my heart rejoiced. The enemy in our lives must be struck with the victory of Jesus, just as the child must receive the necessary physical punishment in order to be corrected. It is easy to shout at your children, but shouting at your children is wrong if they really need the stick, but in love. Our children must wake up spiritually so that the enemy in them withdraws and they become servants of God. It is no good lamenting over your failures and weaknesses in prayer or otherwise. The enemy must be hit directly if he is to withdraw from you. He hit directly saying, *"You are the man"* (see II Samuel 12:7). David then broke down and confessed, *"I have sinned..."* I do not want to beat around the bush, either: You are the man, you are the woman, who is wasting the victorious power of Jesus which is at your disposal. Why, then, is there no revival in your life? Today if you will hear His voice, harden not your hearts!

I am so thankful for the words of Ephesians 6:13-18, *"Wherefore take unto you the whole armour of God, that ye may be able to withstand in the evil day, and having done all, to stand. Stand therefore, having your loins girt about with truth, and having on the breastplate of righteousness; and your feet shod with the preparation of the gospel of peace; above all, taking the shield of faith, wherewith ye shall be able to quench all the fiery darts of the wicked. And take the helmet of salvation, and the sword of the Spirit, which is the Word of God: praying always with all prayer and supplication in the Spirit, and watching thereunto with all perseverance and supplication for all saints."*

What mighty power there is in the wonderful victory of Jesus and through His blood! Let us strike at the enemy where he rules in our life. This means, bring to the light what you have kept back up till now.

The Arabs could have completed their

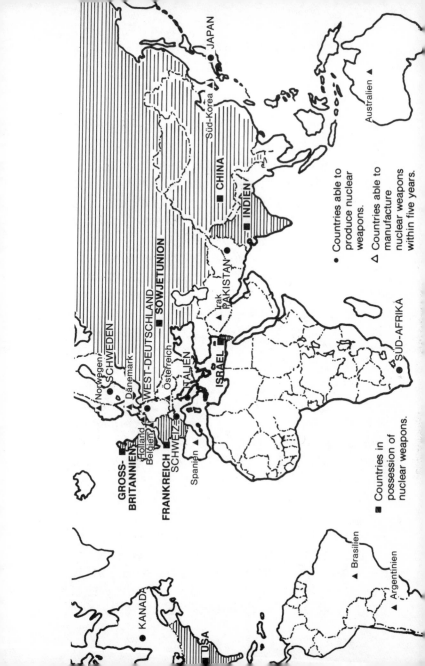

JAPAN ▲

Australien ▲

- Countries able to produce nuclear weapons.
△ Countries able to manufacture nuclear weapons within five years.

Süd-Korea ▲

CHINA ■

INDIEN ■

PAKISTAN ●

Irak ▲

SÜD-AFRIKA ●

ISRAEL ■

ITALIEN ▲

Österreich

Spanien ▲

SCHWEIZ ▲

Norwegen ▲
SCHWEDEN ■

Dänemark

WEST-DEUTSCHLAND ■

SOWJETUNION ■

FRANKREICH ■

Holland
Belgien ▲

GROSS-
BRITANNIEN ■

- Countries in possession of nuclear weapons. ■

KANADA ●

Brasilien ▲

Argentinien ▲

USA ■

preparations for the atom bomb outside Baghdad without anyone taking any notice. Every now and again there were reports about it in the press, but all eyes were directed toward the missiles in Lebanon. But Israel looked further. She brought it to the light and destroyed it.

In order that we can learn the positive side of this lesson, I want to quote I Corinthians 9:24-27, *"Know ye not that they which run in a race run all, but one receiveth the prize? So run, that ye may obtain. And every man that striveth for the mastery, is temperate in all things. Now they do it to obtain a corruptible crown; but we an incorruptible. I therefore so run not as uncertainly; so fight I, not as one that beateth the air: but I keep under my body, and bring it into subjection: lest that by any means, when I have preached to others, I myself should be a castaway."* We must not continue "beating the air," because the enemy in your life has already been beaten by Jesus. Just strike at him in those particular instances in your life, bring the hidden unforgiven sins, the things that bind you, to the light. When you do that, the enemy that binds you will be destroyed. For *"if the Son therefore shall make you free, ye shall be free indeed"* (John 8:36).

Let me conclude with the Lord's own words to us in Revelation 2:29: *"He that has an ear, let him hear what the Spirit saith to the churches."* The Holy Spirit is also saying much through these prophetic events in and around Israel today! *"Seek ye the Lord while he may be found, call ye upon him while he is near"* (Isaiah 55:6).

Midnight Call *Magazine*

This unique and prophetic magazine enlightens the present-day fulfillment of Biblical prophecy. Very helpful and informative articles each month. In short, it is Spiritually packed, challenging, informative, uplifting, and Christ-centered! No serious Christian should be without it. *Midnight Call* helps you to see God's plan clearly for today *and* tomorrow. For your one-year subscription, 12 issues, send $5.00 to:

MIDNIGHT CALL
P.O. Box 864
Columbia, South Carolina 29202

Israel Lightening Strike:
Iraq's Nuclear Reactor Destroyed
America's AWACS Unable to Detect Planes
The World Protests
SPECIAL REPORT ON PAGE 28

News From Israel

July 1981   55¢

News From Israel

This 32-page monthly magazine features articles written by the author of this book, Dr. Wim Malgo. It Biblically attempts to explain the relationship between Israel, the church, and their position in today's world. Many news features illuminated by God's Word in each issue makes this the magazine our subscribers READ from cover to cover. For your one-year subscription, send $5.00 to: **NEWS FROM ISRAEL**
P.O. Box 864
Columbia, South Carolina 29202

For your convenience, there is an order coupon on the last two pages of this book.

By The Same Author...

There Shall Be Signs from 1948-1982

Wim Malgo   **$3.95**

"There shall be signs in the sun, and in the moon, and in the stars, and upon the earth distress among nations." These words spoken by our Lord Jesus Christ in Jerusalem, Israel are the basis of this book.

What are these signs? Could the alignment of the planets, predicted by scientists for 1982, be part of the fulfillment?

Be sure to order this truly fascinating end-time book today! Order extra copies for friends and relatives!

2 books: $6.00   **4 books: $10.00**

Russia's Last Invasion

Wim Malgo   **$3.95**

When will it happen? *"In the latter years thou shalt come into the land that is brought back from the sword, and is gathered out of many people, against the mountains of Israel"* (Ezekiel 38:8). From these immovable statements, the author shows in unmistakably clear terms, how the latest world political movements are developing exactly according to the prophetic statements of the Bible.

2 books: $6.00   **4 books: $10.00**

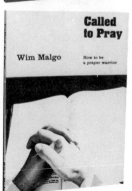

Called to Pray

Wim Malgo   **$3.95**

An enlightening and reliable guide to a victorious prayer-life. Read in this book how Prophets, Apostles, Priests and Kings used PRAYER to overcome the enemy. Tells how your life in Christ can become a powerful testimony. PRAYER is one of the most important subjects in your Bible. 17 inspiring chapters to fill your heart! A real treasure in every Christian home.

2 books: $6.00   **4 books: $10.00**

Biblical Counseling

Wim Malgo   **$4.95**

Biblical Counseling is the title of Dr. Malgo's book containing over 260 questions and answers selected from his 30 years of Counseling Ministry. This book is highly recommended for Ministers, Counselors, and serious Christians. It makes an ideal gift for any occasion. Order extra copies today!

2 books: $8.00   **4 books: $14.00**

Israel Shall Do Valiantly

Wim Malgo   **$3.95**

A book which makes Prophecy come alive! Over 3400 years ago it was said: "Israel Shall Do Valiantly." Today this Prophecy has become a visible reality in the Middle East. Wim Malgo expounds Biblically the Holy Land and it's people from the old past to the present and into the future. Israel, the uncomparable and most astonishing nation of this century. Some of the chapters in this book include...Israel's origin, calling, tragedy and future...Russia's miscalculation and Israel...The connection between space travel, nuclear threat and Israel...Is the Antichrist already among us?...The last two witnesses before worldwide catastrophe...and other vital subjects.

2 books: $6.00   **4 books: $10.00**

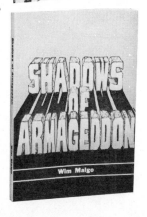

Shadows of Armageddon

Wim Malgo   **$4.95**

What began in 1948 in the Middle East as a seemingly insignificant local matter has taken on worldwide proportions today. The author shows in unmistakably clear terms that even political conflicts such as Vietnam and Cyprus are definitely signs of the preparation for the battle of Armageddon.

2 books: $8.00   **4 books: $14.00**

ORDER FORM

Fill in, Clip and Mail This Whole Page To:

Midnight Call, P.O. Box 864, Columbia, SC 29202